MW01635863

Eyewitness Christmas

A Candle Star Christmas Production: Plays for Churches and Schools

by Shell Isenhoff

ISBN: 978-1470186586

Cover image by Joe Buckingham

Candle Star Press
www.michelleisenhoff.com

A Note to Directors:

Thank you for choosing to use a *Candle Star Christmas Production* in your church or school. My purpose in writing each play was to create a pageant that even small groups could produce simply. (They have all been produced in my own church of 200 people.) But stronger still was my desire to immerse viewers in a powerful story that left no question about the true meaning of Christmas. Christ's coming to dwell with man was only part of the whole gospel message, which is clearly presented in each script.

Other *Candle Star Christmas Productions* are available to preview in their entirety as digital downloads on my website. (Links are provided to free software for viewing on a pc for those without ereaders.) Please respect copyrights. Reproduction rights are granted for each purchasing organization only with paperback versions.

Merry Christmas and break a leg! And to Jesus Christ be all the glory.

Sincerely,
Shell Isenhoff

www.michelleisenhoff.com

Find additional
Candle Star Christmas Productions
on my website:

www.michelleisenhoff.com

.

Table of Contents

Eyewitness Christmas
Plot Summary

In a humorous blend of biblical and modern culture, an aspiring journalist named Luke is trying to break into the periodical, *National Scroll*, with a fantasy Christmas article, but editor Liebowitz rejects it, demanding facts and authenticity. In a second attempt, Luke conducts four interviews to learn exactly what happened that first Christmas night. What he discovers changes everything.

Length

Candle Star Christmas Productions are designed to run between 45 minutes to an hour when music is included at scene breaks.

Cast of Characters

Narrator

Luke: A young aspiring journalist

Editor Liebowitz: Editor of the periodical, *National Scroll*
(He can affect a funny Jewish accent, if desired.)

Betty: A geriatric Bethlehem innkeeper

Pythagorean: A highly educated wise man

Boswell: The red-neck sheep

Mathias: a shepherd

Minimal Prop List

A small table that will seat two people

2 chairs

A "recording device" (this can be the actual microphone)

A lamp

A sheaf of ten or twelve papers that is Luke's "manuscript"

A small, rolled-up paper which is Mathias' "pocket testament" scroll

A pen and paper

Costuming

All characters but the sheep can be dressed in simple Bible-era costumes. Or they could be dressed in a more modern manner to fit their stereotypes.

Sheep costumes may be purchased commercially, but a creative member of your organization might fashion simple ears out of a headband, felt and cotton balls.

Eyewitness Christmas

by Shell Isenhoff

Scene One

Luke is seated on left side of the table, Liebowitz on the right.

Luke Do I get the job, editor Liebowitz?

Liebowitz So, you want for me to hire you to write for the *National Scroll*, but you give me such rubbish to print? And for Christmas?

Luke Well, I thought to draw in a larger audience. Children perhaps.

Liebowitz Little men in red suits, flying donkeys…bah! (*He tosses the manuscript.*) A journalist you are not! You need facts, eyewitnesses! Then produce for me a story that will touch the heart of your readers! This, this *embarrassment* is not worth the sheepskin to write it on!

Luke (*Thoughtfully*) Eyewitnesses. Hmmm…

Optional break for music.

Scene Two

Luke now sits on the right side of the table. He'll stay there till the last scene. Betty knocks, enters, and sits opposite.

Luke Please state your name and occupation into the microphone.

Betty taps it.

Luke It's just a recording device, ma'am. For your story.

Betty Oh, the gadgets young people think they need these days. Why, I remember when I was a girl…

Luke Ma'am, your name?

Betty Oh, yes. Silly me. I'm Betty. I run the Sleep Cheap Inn in Bethlehem. At least I did until I burned it down. And then my kids decided it was time to stick me away in this rest home. (*Spoken as an aside*) I think I'm the only one there who isn't crazy. But they do serve us a mean chocolate pudding in the evenings…

Luke Betty, will you please tell me what you remember of the original Christmas night?

Betty Let's see…that was the middle of the census, right? Whale of a busy week. Good ol' Caesar Augustus, making extra work for an old woman while he's being waited on hand and foot in his palace.

Luke Do you recall the couple expecting the baby?

Betty Oh, yes. I remember them. It's a shame, these unmarried young folks these days getting the cart before the horse.

Luke No, ma'am. You misunderstand. The virgin Mary…

Betty (*Snorts*) She didn't look like no virgin I've ever seen. Anyway, I was full up, but I sent them out back to the barn. Felt sorry for the gal. I remember carrying my own young ones. Right about that ninth month you start thinking the farmers are gunna paint you red.

Luke The baby, ma'am…

Betty Oh, yes, the baby. He made an appearance that night. Can't stop these things, you know. He was a loud one too. Nice set of lungs. Could hear him in the house. I always like a loud baby. Indication of good health. Take my Levi, for instance…

Luke But wasn't there anything unusual about his birth?

Betty Nope, nope. Except he got a lot of visitors real late at night. They came whooping up the road waking everybody up. They all crowded into my barn. Every last one of them. Not sure what they were doing out there.

Luke Didn't you go out to investigate?

Betty Naw, I needed my beauty sleep. Fifteen extra people to cook for, thanks to that no good Caesar. And I knew the lines at the market would be…

Luke Thank you, Betty. You've been so helpful.

Exit Betty.

Luke Nice lady, but a few donuts shy of a dozen. I need a more reliable source. Perhaps someone a bit more intelligent…

Optional break for music.

Scene Three

Pythagorean knocks, enters, and sits.

Luke Please state your name and occupation into the microphone.

Pythagorean My appellative is Pythagorean, my livelihood incorporates the systematic application of knowledge.

Luke You're a wise man?

Pythag Precisely. (*Pointing out microphone*) Your documentation devise appears substandard. This model has been superseded by the Xonic 785, with greater reception and enhanced reverberation.

Luke Uh, I'll look into that. So, Mr. Pythagorean, can you tell me what you remember about the first Christmas?

Pythag A stellar apparition appeared approximately 18 degrees west, southwest.

Luke A star?

Pythag Affirmative. My colleagues and I, upon deciphering its significance, traveled 2,547 miles, that's 4,245 kilometers if you prefer, to reverence the young Jewish Messiah, of whom ancient prophecy foretold. A journey which encompassed 837 days, 13 hours and…

Luke There was a prophecy about the baby?

Pythag Approximately 324.

Luke No kidding. Did you see the baby?

Pythag Affirmative. However, the earth achieved two complete orbits by the conclusion of our expedition.

Luke Of course. Your journey took two years.

Pythag Correct. Unfortunately, maximum sustained camel locomotion registers a mere 3 miles per hour, or if you prefer, that's 5…

Luke …kilometers an hour. Yes, yes. Thank you so much for your time, Mr. Pythagorean, but I really need someone who was there that first night.

Optional break for music.

Scene Four

Boswell knocks, enters, and sits.

Luke Please state your name and occupation into the microphone.

Boswell My name's Boswell. Um, I'm a sheep.

Luke Thank you, Boswell. I understand you were on the Judean hillside on Christmas night. Can you please describe it for me?

Boswell Well it started out pretty normal. The shepherds were sitting around their fire. The wife and I were happily sharing a salad (*becomes animated*) when all of a sudden a whole swarm of the biggest fireflies I have ever scene lit up the entire sky. Were talking steroids here!

Luke So there *were* angels!

Boswell Call them what you want, they scared the ba-jeebers out of me.

Luke What happened?

Boswell Well, they were kind of hovering around, singing and talking and stuff. And then, the shepherds just all took off running! They just left us. I tell you, the quality of my wool ain't been the same. I mean, how were we to know the fireflies weren't coming back? How could we know these weren't flesh-eating fireflies?

Luke Where did the shepherds go?

Boswell And my poor wife, she won't even leave the fold anymore. She's terrified of bugs.

Luke Did they find the baby?

Boswell And that's a terrible phobia when you smell like a sheep. If a fly even comes in the door, why she starts…

Luke (*Sarcastically*) Thank you, Boswell. You've been a tremendous help. (*Boswell exits.*) Give my regards to your missus.

Luke (*Acting out extreme frustration*) I don't think I'm cut out for this profession.

Luke drops head face down on table and remains like that until the next scene.

Optional break for music.

Scene 5

Mathias knocks, enters, and sits.

Luke (*Weary, resigned, hopeless, still face down*) Please state your name and occupation into the microphone.

Mathias I'm Mathias, I'm a shepherd.

Luke (*Lifting head, but half-hearted*) Mathias, can you recall any events from the first Christmas night?

Mathias Can I recall them? Son, I will never forget them. They changed my life.

Luke (*Showing some interest*) How?

Mathias Ah, to understand that, you must know what I once was. My heart was black. Full of anger, curses, secrets. The rabbis spoke of a Messiah. But rabbis care nothing for shepherds. And their Messiah, I thought, would not trouble himself with one as lowly as I.

But that blessed night the angels appeared, not in the synagogue of the rabbis, but on a dark hillside full of sheep and dirty men, and they invited us to the birthplace of God's Son!

We found the child, just as the angels said; a precious, fragile, nursing infant, tiny as a spring lamb. He lay beside his exhausted mother in the hay of a stable. But that night, that stable was a tabernacle, for the presence of God was there. And as I knelt in the dirt beside that manger, my darkness fell away, because at last, I understood that God's love reaches not only to rabbis, but to lowly shepherds.

Luke Do you think it extends to discouraged reporters as well?

Mathias Son, it's the greatest love you'll ever know. Let me show you…(*Takes out a "pocket testament" scroll and pantomime evangelism as lights go out.*)

Lights out. Mathias exits. Luke sits alone on stage.

No break for music.

Scene 6

Stage is dark. Luke clicks on lamp and sits "writing" Luke 2:1-20 (NIV, 1984) as it is read out loud over the sound system by the Narrator.

1 In those days Caesar Augustus issued a decree that a census should be
taken of the entire Roman world. 2 (This was the first census that took place
while Quirinius was governor of Syria.) 3 And everyone went to his own town
to register.

4 So Joseph also went up from the town of Nazareth in Galilee to Judea, to
Bethlehem the town of David, because he belonged to the house and line of
David. 5 He went there to register with Mary, who was pledged to be married
to him and was expecting a child. 6 While they were there, the time came for
the baby to be born, 7 and she gave birth to her firstborn, a son. She
wrapped him in cloths and placed him in a manger, because there was no
room for them in the inn.

8 And there were shepherds living out in the fields nearby, keeping watch
over their flocks at night. 9 An angel of the Lord appeared to them, and the
glory of the Lord shone around them, and they were terrified. 10 But the
angel said to them, "Do not be afraid. I bring you good news of great joy
that will be for all the people. 11 Today in the town of David a Savior has
been born to you; he is Christ the Lord. 12 This will be a sign to you: You will
find a baby wrapped in cloths and lying in a manger."

13 Suddenly a great company of the heavenly host appeared with the angel,
praising God and saying,

14 "Glory to God in the highest,
and on earth peace to men on whom his favor rests."

15 When the angels had left them and gone into heaven, the shepherds said
to one another, "Let's go to Bethlehem and see this thing that has
happened, which the Lord has told us about."

16 So they hurried off and found Mary and Joseph, and the baby, who was
lying in the manger. 17 When they had seen him, they spread the word
concerning what had been told them about this child, 18 and all who heard it
were amazed at what the shepherds said to them. 19 But Mary treasured up
all these things and pondered them in her heart. 20 The shepherds returned,
glorifying and praising God for all the things they had heard and seen, which
were just as they had been told.

Play or perform closing song – All is Well, *by Wayne Kirkpatrick and Michael W. Smith.*

At this point, you may wish to give your minister a few moments to address the audience.

Scene Seven

Back in Liebowitz's office, Luke is seated on left side of the table. Liebowitz on right.

Liebowitz Beautiful! Astonishing! Heartrending! Son, can I expect more reporting of this caliber from you in the future?

Luke Sorry, sir. You were right. I'm no journalist. (*He stands.*) I've enrolled in medical school. I've decided to become… a doctor!

Music Recommendations

At the end of most scenes, an option break for music is inserted. This is left wide open on purpose, because the organizations that produce this play will have vastly different musical talents available. They may even choose to skip some or all of these opportunities. However, music offers a great distraction while switching scenes, and it provides a whole additional platform for worship. Here is a list of suggestions to fill these opportunities:

Songs sung by children's Sunday school classes or school classrooms

Vocal solos or groups performed by children or adults

Instrumental solos performed by school children or adults

Brief piano interludes

Traditional carols provide simple, recognizable tunes for instrumentals. Vocal arrangements might consist of carols as well, or be drawn from the variety of contemporary music available.

All is Well, written by Wayne Kirkpatrick and Michael W. Smith, makes a powerful conclusion to this play. It is available commercially by a variety of artists. The "canned" version may be played over the sound system, or it can be performed live by members of your organization.

Made in the USA
San Bernardino, CA
25 August 2015